# JIU-JITSU
# *SELLING*

## WHITE BELT: INTRO

**Escaping Objections, Blocking Negativity,
& Guarding Rapport**

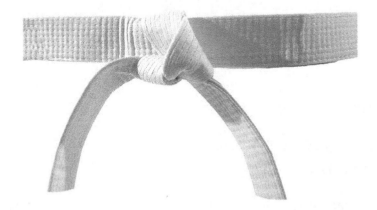

## BY FRITZ SATTES

ISBN: 978-1-7353771-0-0

## THIS SERIES IS DEDICATED TO:

My Parents for giving me all,

My Godparents for teaching me everything in these books, for their guidance, and for providing me the opportunities to prove, build, and refine them,

And to my Wife and Sons for motivating me to write them and supporting me throughout the process.

Thank You and I Love You!!

# WHAT IS JIU-JITSU SELLING?

The Jiu Jitsu Selling program is totally unlike any other sales training. It gives you a clear understanding of sales and the skills required to navigate the sales process successfully; it's what the other gurus promised but didn't deliver. Here are the three main differences:

**First, it's the only complete system ever produced.**

I've studied hundreds of books, audio programs, and classes on sales. Each of them promoted their own angle on how best to sell; frankly, they were all pretty much the same. They solely addressed selling behavior, and not one of them accounted for how people buy, so they were missing half the equation. Half! You wouldn't want to go to space with math like that, would you?

Think of it like a football team who only focuses on offense. On the chalkboard, all their plays appear to work every time, but when they get on the field, they find things hardly ever work out the way they planned. That's because they didn't factor in the other team's defense when determining the effectiveness of their offense. Ignoring the fact that the Prospect will actively try to stop you at every step is delusional. It's just not operating in reality.

The correct formula accounts for buying as well. Both sides of the equation must balance for the system to work. It is just as important for you to know how people buy as it is for you to know how to sell properly. In fact, the former dictates the latter.

You must always account for buying behavior, or you will consistently create your own sales resistance, and you'll never completely understand sales.

### Second, anyone can do it.

Jiu-Jitsu means "soft art" which is the opposite of all other martial arts, and by extension, other sales programs. What are other sales programs? Hard, abrasive, rushed, and pushy. These are adjectives normally associated with selling, and nobody wants to be pegged as a Salesperson. Besides these monikers, there is an inherent accusation of dishonesty applied to people who choose to communicate this way.

Our program is *soft*. It doesn't feel like sales, so it doesn't meet with intense resistance, and therefore doesn't require great strength.

Jiu Jitsu was designed to enable a smaller person to beat a larger, stronger opponent. Accordingly, I designed my system to make you effective without requiring you to be superior to your Prospect. You don't need to know everything about his business, you don't need to make more money than he does, you don't need to wield more influence, and you don't need to have some inside track that gives you an edge. You don't need to be an experienced Salesperson or to be morally flexible. You don't even need to be particularly intelligent. Anyone can use these techniques with any person in any situation.

I have been a Field Sales Trainer for over 30 years and have trained thousands of Salespeople across 49 states and in 12 countries. I'm not hoping, predicting, or guessing this works. It absolutely does, regardless of your age, race, gender, height, hairline, weight, religion, political affiliation, experience, what you're selling, or where you're selling it; it doesn't matter and it never has.

All the people I have trained, to a person, were able to understand it and apply it. It increased not only their sales, but the ease with which those sales came. Plus, it dramatically reduced negativity and lifted the positive responses the Salespeople received throughout the selling process.

Unlike outdated techniques and canned lines that don't fit your personality, don't apply to your industry, or aren't easy to duplicate, these skills are completely transferrable. When they are employed correctly, they are irresistible, imperceptible, and inexhaustible.

**Third, this is the most comprehensive training available.**

Whether you're a seasoned sales professional or a blank slate, this program will take you from zero to hero. In fact, it's better if you have no training at all, because you won't have to unlearn the self-defeating stratagem that burdens you.

Throughout this 5-belt series, we'll take you from the fundamentals of communication and objection handling, to proficient prospecting and presenting, then we'll hone these skills as you craft your own personal style. We finish by guiding your rise from Salesperson to Sales Manager.

This series is divided into five belts. There are several parts to each belt, mirroring the belt grades in Jiu-Jitsu. The following is a brief overview of this level and the four that follow.

## WHITE BELT OVERVIEW

This first level is the White Belt level training. In the sport of Jiu Jitsu, the goal of the White Belt is survival: not putting yourself in a bad position, and escaping the bad positions your opponent places you in. We teach no offensive techniques; rather, you will learn how to defend attacks and prevent making the kinds of mistakes that make recovery difficult.

Most lost sales begin breaking down due to the Salesperson having poor communication and initial contact skills. This holds true across all levels of Salespeople. We address these skills, because to ignore them guarantees we lose a certain percentage of sales. This is unacceptable because our behavior is the one thing we absolutely can control.

Something we can't control is that people don't always agree with us, so we teach objection handling at this level too, using the theory of **Negative-Neutral-Positive**, or NNP. Rather than beat the Prospect in an argument over his objection, NNP guides him down a path where he, of his own accord, decides to correct and refine his opinion on a given subject.

Besides being the ultimate objection handling formula, NNP can be extended to prevent objections from arising, lower sales resistance, and even create sales attraction, which we will see in our subsequent books.

Once you learn this simple two-step process, you will use it for the rest of your life, both socially and in business.

(THIS BOOK IS PART ONE OF THREE PARTS/BOOKS IN THE WHITE BELT LEVEL)

## BLUE BELT OVERVIEW

The second level, Blue Belt, is about putting yourself into a position to win and setting up a base from which you can comfortably begin to launch your offense. In sales, this translates to crafting a proper first impression and prospecting effectively.

Most Salespeople calling on your Prospects are like Frankenstein walking their way through a series of predictable sales steps to which the Prospect is already predisposed to resist. By following a rigid prospecting formula, your competitors are working hard to fit into the herd, and they will be culled accordingly. That approach in itself implies that Salespeople have a selfish goal in mind: to get the appointment and subsequently to get the sale. This is Pushing.

I often ask trainees, "What is the goal of prospecting?" and they invariably answer, "To set the appointment." This is incorrect.

The goal of prospecting is the creation of rapport. Rapport is never resisted and usually results in the setting of an appointment. This is Pulling.

You will learn the **Fishing Theory**, our prospecting method, which results in the kind of appointment the Prospect will anticipate. When we set a good appointment, we will make the sale, but when we set a shaky appointment, we wonder if the guy is even going to show. Your goal is to set solid appointments because this is when the sale begins, not at the presentation.

(THERE ARE 3 PARTS/BOOKS IN THE BLUE BELT LEVEL)

## PURPLE BELT OVERVIEW

The Purple Belt level in Jiu Jitsu is when you start working on your offense. For us, this means presenting and client retention.

For most of you, your presentation training consisted of receiving a presentation book or a bunch of fliers and a rate card. Your manager told you to point, read it out loud, then ask for the close. By the way, here are a couple answers to the objections you're going to get. Good luck. Then you go out, try it a few times, and start cutting the parts your Prospects don't seem to care about. Pretty soon, you're left with a rate card you don't adhere to anyway.

Well, buddy, that ain't gonna cut it.

First, you need to understand how people buy. A Prospect is always capable of resisting a sales techniques when motivated, but they cannot resist their own buyer's path. To them, saying yes is the same thing as making a good decision.

We'll show you how to leverage your prospecting into the presentation, so your Prospect is motivated. Then we'll order the information in the presentation according to Maslow's Hierarchy of Needs with our **Bridge Theory**, and we'll show you how to use your rate card as a tool, which it is.

What am I missing? The close?

Nope. To be clear, our presentation guides the Prospect's buying behavior, and there is no Closing. Why? Because the natural result of a proper presentation is that the *Buyer* asks for the sale. Remember, we are pulling, not pushing the Prospect.

I know this is a relief to many of you, and some of you aren't quite ready to believe it, but yes, it's true: there is no need for closing techniques in my system.

(THERE ARE 3 PARTS/BOOKS IN THE PURPLE BELT LEVEL)

## BROWN BELT OVERVIEW

Part Four is the Brown Belt level when the student knows all the attacks and defenses and is better at some of the moves but not as good at the others. This stage of development in sport Jiu Jitsu is focused on the refinement of technique: making each movement more subtle, effective, and effortless. Similarly, this section in Jiu Jitsu selling is all about style.

Style is the music of your life. It is how you feel, and it has the power to influence others' feelings as well. It is the ease with which you operate, the power behind your movements, and the direction of your destiny: the attainment of results without the appearance of strife.

Picture all your activities, efforts, and personality traits like oarsmen on a large ship. The development of your style is nothing more than the synchronization of the rowing in every way: timing, depth, length, and direction. The more aligned all these energies are, the smoother and easier the progress is and the more assured you are of reaching your destination.

There is nothing fake or phony about this process. Quite the opposite. It demands great emotional courage on your part.

We will methodically walk you through a deep self-examination to empower you to deliberately craft your avatar, we will help you lift your **Emotional Quotient** to ease your interactions and lower your negative reactions. We will also discuss pragmatically crucial trainings relating to body language, gender, multi-cultural differences, and multi-generational sales, which are often viewed as being too controversial to discuss.

When you have reached even a cursory level of competence in this section, you will have an enhanced sense of control of your life.

## BLACK BELT OVERVIEW

Finally, the fifth book, Black Belt, guides your rise from student to teacher, from Salesperson to Sales Manager.

Most companies would love to promote from within because there are so many benefits to this policy. The manager already knows the product, is proficient in the sales system, and understands the market and all the players in the company. Plus, a reputation for promoting from within attracts higher-quality candidates to the company which strengthens it at all levels.

Unfortunately, the downsides of moving a Salesrep into management typically outweigh the upsides. The new Manager has a difficult time wearing the mantle of authority, because their former peers still view them as friends, are jealous, and perhaps have some dirt on them.

Familiarity does breed contempt, and for this reason, you will almost always will see a decline in morale and productivity.

Bottom line: being a great Salesperson has little to do with being a competent Manager. There are few transferrable skills, and this is why companies look outside for professional management.

With proper training and a transition plan supported by upper management, a Salesperson can quickly and effectively rise to the ranks of Sales Manager and become an even greater asset to the company.

# WHITE BELT: INTRO

## Escaping Objections, Blocking Negativity, & Guarding Rapport

Does this conversation sound familiar?

**Prospect**- "I'm not buying from you because your advertising is too expensive."

**Salesperson**- "Cheap is good, but good isn't cheap. We have the highest quality, so it's worth more."

**Prospect**- "I don't care. You're still too expensive."

**Salesperson**- "What is truly expensive is making a poor decision. Experience counts in this business. We've been around the longest, so we know what we're doing."

**Prospect**- "I'm just not interested right now. Check back with me in the fall."

**Salesperson**- "I can't guarantee this special price will still be available then. If it's a good decision in the fall, then it's a better decision now at the lower price."

**Prospect**- "Look, you're not listening to me. I am not interested, and if the rate you're going to offer me next fall is higher, don't even bother following up with me. You're just overpriced."

**Salesperson**- "I'm amazed you feel that way. I think we have the best value proposition in the market. Let's back up and review some of the key points."

**Prospect**- "Let's not. Please leave."

Have you ever had a conversation like this?

Sure, we all have. It's called an argument, and it doesn't matter who is arguing or what they are arguing about. The pattern is universal, and the pattern is the problem, not the issues that arise. Let's examine what's happening here.

The Salesguy is busy telling the prospect why buying from him is a good decision, and the Prospect is busy telling the Salesperson why buying from him is a bad decision. Each is pushing his point of view onto the other person. The energy is going outward, almost as if each person is physically pushing the other. It feels like pushing because they are talking, telling, explaining, asserting, defending, advocating, and neither party is doing what? Listening! Even though the Salesperson *wants* to form a bond, because he is pushing while the Prospect is also pushing, he only succeeds in creating more distance between himself and the sale.

## Sales Magnet

This is like how magnets behave when two like poles are facing each other. What happens?

They repel each other.

You can make them appear to bond by forcing them together. They may be touching, but they will not have made a connection. They will be closer but will not have made any progress. When you let go, what happens?

They fly apart.

This physical response between the magnets is mirrored in the psychological response created when both parties in a conversation are pushing. It is the definition of "repulsion." This repulsion is natural, so you yield the same result no matter how many times you try, and this repulsion is everlasting.

In this example, and to the Salesperson's discredit, he persists in his attempt to sell. He's trying to force the two parties together. In keeping with the analogy, he's trying to force one magnet to embrace the other. This is known as **Sales Pressure**. Although it may appear he's getting closer to the sale, he's really only amplifying **Buyer's Resistance** on the part of the Prospect. Initially, the Prospect may have been simply disinterested or cautious, but now he is emotionally invested in denying this sale. He actively dislikes the Salesperson.

**LAW #1:**
They don't have to like you to do business with you, but they will make every attempt not to do business with you if they dislike you.

**LAW #2:**
You can't win a sale by winning an argument. If you're arguing, you've already lost the sale.

## NEGATIVE-NEUTRAL-POSITIVE

Negative-Neutral-Positive, or NNP for short, was introduced to me as an objection-handling formula. It is a superior method to traditional sales theory because it considers how people make decisions. NNP guides the Prospect through this process as opposed to other popular methods which are more geared towards making Prospects submit even when they still harbor concerns.

Take a look at the picture below. This seesaw represents the Prospect's inclination to buy or not to buy. Right now, he's leaning towards not buying as he only has one piece of information about what you are selling, and it is negative. That's the circle with a line through it.

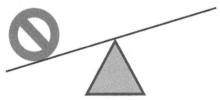

Traditional sales theory instructs us to forget about that negative and focus on the other side of the seesaw by loading it up with positives, or reasons to buy, in the hopes of tipping the scale in our favor. Those are the plus symbols.

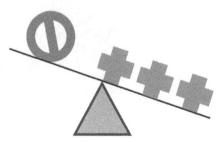

The picture above is what they told you would happen, and the one below is what actually does happen. The Prospect is still opposed to the sale, because the positives slid right off the seesaw and never made it into the Prospect's consideration process.

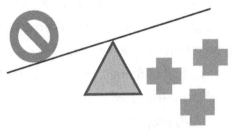

"WHY?!" you ask.

"Yeah but," that's why.

Let's back up. The Prospect rejected the sale and you asked why. Out of the kindness of his heart, he shared his objection with you. Instead of addressing his concern, you ignored it and said, "Yeah, but this. Yeah, but that, and yeah, but the other thing."

You piled on a bunch of unrelated selling points, none of which affected the validity of his objection, so the objection persisted. You proved you weren't listening to him, that you really don't care about him or his business, and that you're only there to line your pockets.

This is what the so-called gurus are missing. If the Prospect has just one reason to oppose the sale, despite all the positive evidence the Salesperson brings, they are still going to be at negative. If there is a problem with the product, then there is a problem with the product.

You can't just bury it and make it go away.

Think of it this way: I want to sell you an airplane. It's practically brand new. It has a custom interior. It looks great, and I'm going to give it to you at cost. There's just one thing: the wings are bent so it can't get airborne without rolling over and crashing into a ball of flames. Wanna buy it? No?

Well, what if I threw in floor mats?

How about a DVD player?

Tinted windows?

Come on. No matter what I add to the sale, it's not going to change the fact that the plane is a death trap. The only way forward with an objection is to remove the negative, or in this case, straighten out the wings. Once I remove the negative, look what happens:

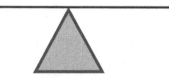

The Prospect is no longer at negative and has moved to a neutral position where he has no opinion one way or the other. Now the Prospect is willing to listen and consider your selling points. Now you can share them, and they won't fall off. Go ahead.

See? Isn't that better?

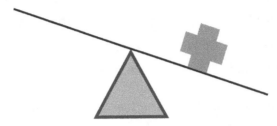

If the Prospect has an objection, he is at negative. He has a reason, or a negative, to object to your point of view. Your aim is to bring him from negative to neutral and then from neutral to positive. That's two steps. It's not just one step from negative to positive, but two steps.

Attempting to go from negative directly to positive, as we've seen in our illustration, doesn't work. When a Prospect is at negative, he will not listen to anything you have to say unless it addresses the concern he just expressed. The more you talk about other features that make your product attractive, the more you sound like Charlie Brown's teacher. He is not listening.

The first step in moving from negative to neutral is when you neutralize, answer, remove, or otherwise satisfy the Prospect's concern. You don't ignore it. You don't change the subject. You address it directly and to his complete satisfaction.

If the Salesperson can remove this negative, the Prospect no longer has a reason to hold a negative attitude towards the sale. He moves into the neutral position, and this is the first time his mind is fallow, or open to new information.

The Prospect has to be at neutral in order to listen what you have to say. That's the only time when you can make your second step from neutral to positive, and that's easy because the Prospect is no longer resisting you. You just do what you normally do and give him a good reason to like your product.

Let's re-run the advertising sales call and see if NNP could have made a difference.

### Successful Example

**Prospect**- "I'm not buying from you because your advertising is too expensive."

**Salesperson**- "Thank you for sharing your concern with me. Tell me, what do you mean by too expensive?"

**Prospect**- "I mean the newspaper delivers to 30,000 homes for what you're charging for 10,000."

**Salesperson**- "I see. So, from your perspective, my competition is offering you three times the value."

**Prospect**- "Exactly."

**Salesperson**- "I understand where you're coming from, and I'd be in agreement with you if I believed circulation equaled audience."

**Prospect**- "What do you mean?"

**Salesperson**- "Your target market is the three-mile radius around this nail salon, and your target audience is upper-income women. Did your newspaper rep break down how many of those 30,000 live within three miles of this store?"

**Prospect-** "Well, no, but I'd imagine quite a few. This is a highly residential area."

**Salesperson-** "You're definitely in a good area; no doubt about it. What percentage of the newspaper's audience matches your high-income female demographic? Did he share that with you?"

**Prospect-** "No. They have that?"

**Salesperson-** "Of course, it's the newspaper. They have all kinds of statistics. Their target audience is white males aged 55 and older which doesn't line up with your needs, and their market is the entire county; most of which is outside your 3-mile radius. That probably explains why there are no other nail salons advertising in the paper."

**Prospect-** "Hmmm."

**Salesperson-** "I'm not trying to slam them. They do a good job, but not every media is a good fit for every business. They have content that I can't hold, and I have content aimed at exactly what you want: upper-income women in your neighborhood. So, do you see how comparing their 30,000 to my 10,000 isn't apples to apples?"

**Prospect-** "Yes, now I do. I probably wouldn't get anything out of the paper. Thank you."

**Salesperson-** "Sure, my pleasure. Has this changed your opinion of my magazine a bit? Ten thousand homes inside of three miles is a pretty good number of potential clients, right?"

**Prospect-** "Yes, it has and, yes, now I am interested."

## Examination

Did that seem like a reasonable scenario? It should. I've seen nearly that exact conversation hundreds of times. In our example, the Salesperson is even a bit gruff.

What just happened here? The Salesperson took away the Prospect's negative, or reason not to buy. This happened in two steps. First, the Salesperson addressed the false impression that circulation equaled target audience. After that, the Prospect was at neutral. He no longer had a reason not to buy. His mind became receptive to new information. This is the point when the Prospect is open to hearing what you have to say. Second, the Salesperson introduced the positive, or reason to buy and got the sale.

Are you starting to feel the Jiu Jitsu vibe here? When the Salesperson gets the objection, instead of blocking the objection, ignoring it, changing the subject, or punching back at the Prospect, he does what? He takes what the Prospect gives him, allowing him to feel comfortable and in control of the conversation, and then slowly educates him which essentially dissolves the complaint.

How do you think the Prospect felt during this process?

Unlike traditional sales theory that promotes a sense of combat and opposition, the magnets have flipped here, haven't they? First off, the Prospect never sensed conflict. The tone was conversational. Second, he is appreciative for having learned something and is most likely feeling confident about his decision to buy advertising.

Something else to point out: when the Prospect arrived at neutral, the power relationship flipped, and the Salesperson became Top Dog. This is one of the hidden benefits of NNP. I gotta tell you: it's pretty satisfying when you get there.

It's not about the words. It's about opening the mind of the Prospect gently and with class. It's not about talking so much as it is about earning the right to speak and motivating the Prospect to listen.

Let me repeat that for full emphasis. It's about *earning* the right to speak, or in other words, it's about motivating the Prospect to listen.

## What if You're Wrong?

Here's an interesting question: "What if you're wrong?"

What if the Prospect's objection turned out to be valid and you were the one with the incorrect or incomplete information?

If you used an objection handling technique like the Salesperson did in the first example, then you've already attacked the Prospect and insulted his intelligence. He is still intellectually opposed to the sale, and likely is emotionally committed to opposing you personally now too.

With NNP, your first move is a question. You don't give away your position, and the Prospect doesn't feel he has to defend against you. You also continue your position as listener, so the Prospect still feels in control and is comfortable. Most importantly, you maintain rapport.

If he is right, he will answer your question and reinforce his position as the man in charge. He feels smart, and guess what? He likes you more now, and you learned something with no downside.

Everyone likes to be right, right? Even if you have to walk away from the sale, you will always be welcomed back, because the Prospect is convinced you put his needs first.

In most martial arts, you are only vulnerable when you attack, because you must abandon a defensive posture when you use that part of your body in the offensive attack. In Jiu Jitsu, you don't attack until you are in an invulnerable position.

The focus is on positioning yourself correctly as opposed to breaking the other person down in a flurry of assaults.

When your focus is on creating the right position, your offense never fails, and you are never wrong. Again, don't focus on the words; focus on the *mindset* of the Prospect. Putting them first, just as you receive a guest into your home, is the epitome of class.

## Gunfight

Here's another scenario to help you picture this exchange of energies and roles formed by NNP.

Handling objections can be likened to a gunfight in the wild west. The reasons supporting your point of view are like the bullets in your gun. You and I are shooting it out. Each of us is behind a big bolder. I have one bullet and you have six. You have the advantage, but it's still a dangerous situation for both of us. One of us could choose to leave the safety of the rock and rush towards the other hoping to get a clear shot off, but it's likely that person will get hurt. We end up in a standoff. Or do we?

What if I could get you to shoot all your bullets while I'm hidden safely behind my boulder? I throw a pebble over your shoulder, you hear it bounce, spin around, and shoot. I prop my cowboy hat up just above my boulder and you take a shot. I smack my horse on the rear, he bolts around creating a smokescreen, and you fire rounds all through it. That would work, right?

I know. You wouldn't shoot, but what if you did? I could then come from behind the rock, stroll over to you, and win the day. That might be unlikely in a gun fight but think about the easiest things to receive on a sales call: reasons not to buy. These are your prospects' bullets, and they'll shoot all of them every last time.

But what if you could handle all the negatives up front? Let's say he shared three valid concerns that caused him to be hesitant to buy what you are selling, and you were able to answer each of these to his complete satisfaction. He had three reasons, no more and no less, and you pacified all of them. How would that change the attitude or energy of the buyer?

His stance would no longer be negative towards you. It would be neutral, and for the first time he would be open to listening to the positives you have to offer. How many bullets do you need to win a gunfight? That's right: only one.

## STAY CALM!

By now, you should have a basic understanding of NNP on an energetic or psychological level. As such, it is currently a blunt instrument in your toolbox. You will need to learn the application of this theory in four steps so you can apply it tactfully. This is what you need to remember: when you receive, or even sense an objection coming over the horizon, remain CALM. C-A-L-M. CALM stands for Clarify, Acknowledge, Lead, and Move On.

- **Clarifying** narrows a vague objection into something specific, so when you answer it, you can hit your target.

- **Acknowledging** validates the Prospect's opinion, which keeps the tone conversational and is key to earning the right to speak.

- **Leading** is answering the objection, which brings them to neutral.

- **Moving On** is the introduction of positives, which progresses the sale with an eye on tempo. This keeps the Prospect "in the mood." If there is no interruption in the rhythm or pace of the meeting, it implies that having concerns is as common in your sales track as making the sale.

Are you seeing NNP baked into this process? Clarifying, Acknowledging, and Leading are how you make the jump from Negative to Neutral, and Moving On is the second step from Neutral to Positive.

## CLARIFY

Let's begin with "C" for Clarify.

If you have been in sales for any amount of time, chances are you have received the price objection: something to the effect of "It costs too much."

If you repeated a point or two from your presentation for your answer, you basically just called the guy stupid to his face. You can't shoot the bullet twice.

If you answered the wrong objection, you confirmed what all buyers suspect about Salespeople: they cannot be trusted because they don't listen.

"How can this be?" you ask.

My answer to you is, "What does 'It costs too much' mean?"

It could mean several different things, couldn't it?

- It could mean "I can't afford it," or "I don't have any money, but don't want to admit it."
- It could also mean "Your competition sells the same thing for less."
- "You're asking for more than what your product/ service is worth."
- "I don't think I'll make a profit on this," or "I won't save enough on this to justify the expense."

- "I'm afraid of making a decision," or "I'm afraid of trying something new."
- "I'm not really the decision-maker."
- "I'm really interested, but I'm trying to negotiate a better rate," and on and on the story goes.

You see, there are Stated Objections and True Objections.

**Stated Objections** are the ones you receive first. They are usually vague because the Prospect is trying to let you down gently, He doesn't want to be specific because he knows you will try to answer the objection, and he just wants this horror show of a sales call to be over.

**True Objections** are the real reasons Prospects don't want to move forward with the sale. They are the ones you get once you have "given permission" to the Prospect to be honest with you as implied indirectly through your tone and directly with your words.

> **LAW #3:**
> If you receive 20 objections from the Prospect, the only *real* one is the 20th.

If you assume you know the true objection and skip the clarification step, you could fire off the greatest response ever spoken and still miss your target. In fact, odds are you will miss your target. You see what I'm getting at here?

Answering the Stated Objection is like trying to punch a cloud. What happens? Your hand goes right through it. To handle this objection cloud, you're going to have to firm it up first. How do we do that?

We clarify it by asking questions. When the Prospect answers the questions, he gives you more information and narrows it down to specifics which unveil the True Objection.

When we skip the Clarification step, we destroy rapport and guarantee we will miss our mark more often than we hit it; both of these are sales killers, but there are positive reasons we should Clarify too.

First, as you now are aware, it narrows the Stated Objection down to the True Objection, which gives you a fair shot at answering it and making the sale.

Second, Clarifying is a component of active listening. When you make a concerted effort to completely understand the Prospect, it is a sign of respect. Although you and the Prospect may currently disagree, you refuse to judge him and still put him above you in the relationship.

You're not mad. You're not disappointed. You are curious and concerned for his benefit. If the Prospect is convinced you are putting his needs first when you gather information, he will anticipate your response. This is the key to earning the right to speak and be heard.

> **LAW #4:**
> Prescription without diagnosis is malpractice.

Third, Clarifying allows the Prospect to hear themselves out loud. This can have a chilling effect in many cases. They may see the folly in their own position and begin backtracking without any effort on your part.

They begin musing audibly in support of your position, filling in gaps with the points you were wanting to say. The next thing you know, they have presented your product to themselves, often eloquently.

> **LAW #5:**
> What you say to them has almost no weight compared to what they say to themselves.

Jiu-Jitsu is the only martial art you can train at full speed without injuring yourself or your partner. Your opponent is using all his skills to make you submit. This can be very stressful when you are new to the sport and find yourself struggling to defend attacks. The struggle itself can make you lose as you can gas out quickly. Later in your training, you will be able to gauge the threat level and will be aware of your defenses. You will learn to relax and roll for the full five-minute rounds.

This is why you should work on your objection-handling game before your other skills. As you become more competent, you will be able to relax when you Prospect and Present, and your air of confidence will suit you well.

Let's return to our example and see how different responses feel.

Here we go: Take One

**Prospect**- "I'm not buying from you because your advertising is too expensive."

**Salesperson**- "Well, if it's profitable, then by definition, it's not too expensive. You should have a fair degree of confidence by now that you will more than make your money back."

I have to admit, way back when, I might have liked this comeback. These days it sounds like something a politician might say when you ask a question and they seem like they're answering it, but they really don't. You can't even remember the question you asked after they're done talking.

Putting that aside, how did it feel? It felt somewhere between sneaky and combative, didn't it? Does it pass the gut check? No.

Now, we have the advantage here because we already know this Prospect's true objection is that he thinks the newspaper delivers three times the value of what the Salesperson is currently offering. Our first observation is that the Salesperson just missed the target. That means he lost the sale.

As you progress through this training, try the mental exercise of envisioning yourself as the Prospect. It's helpful to develop empathy so you know how your Prospect feels.

If you're the Prospect, you've just given the Salesperson an objection. He's getting all defensive, acting like you're accusing him of trying to sell you something that doesn't work. It's not that. You just don't want to pay three times too much.

Let's go again: Take Two

**Prospect-** "I'm not buying from you because your advertising is too expensive."

**Salesperson-** "I can see how you might have a little sticker shock out of the gate, but we advertise for a lot of businesses in your category and have for years, so chances are, you'll make some money with us."

**Prospect-** "Really?! Just how many of my competitors are going to be in this next issue?"

Oops, he really stepped in it this time, didn't he? Not only did he miss his target, but he just introduced an *additional* reason for the Prospect to oppose the sale: the fact that his response rate will be watered down in the advertising pool.

You want your Prospect to know that businesses in his category do have success with you, but you don't want to introduce yet another reason not to buy. In NNP, we call this "shooting yourself in the foot."

I'd ask you to give this a gut check rating, but I think we all know the feeling is embarrassment.

Last example: Take Three

**Prospect-** "I'm not buying from you because your advertising is too expensive."

**Salesperson-** "If your measurement is cost per qualified impression, it is actually the cheapest media out there, because our readers fit your target audience. The newspaper almost completely misses it."

Curveball! You didn't expect the Salesman would guess the correct objection this time, did you? Look, we all guess right *some* of the time. What I want you to understand is how the Prospect feels even when you get it right.

The Prospect might say, "So buying a newspaper ad makes me stupid?"

He could. He might be offended you criticized his decision, or maybe he just feels your response was argumentative.

What is your gut telling you now? I know, you want to stand up for the noble Salesman, because he and all of us take too much grief from Prospects. I get it. He's speaking truth to power like the hero Spartacus, but what have I been telling you here?

We're not fighting back against the *oppressor*. We're trying to communicate more effectively. Bouncing back is argumentative. It destroys rapport and injures the sale.

In this example, the Prospect is still not ready to listen, which is our primary goal in objection handling. He may engage you because he doesn't want to lose an argument, but you have just made yourself the issue instead of the product you're representing, and that is a mistake.

**LAW #6:**
Never answer the first, or Stated, objection without clarifying it, even if you are convinced you know what the True objection is.

Before we continue, I'd like to point out the obvious fact that not everyone will react so negatively, nor will they read into comments so deeply and quickly. But what is our goal at the white belt level? It's survival, not putting ourselves in a bad or vulnerable position. To that end, when we eradicate as many landmines in our approach as possible, we do what?

We maximize our potential sales and the ease with which they come. When the sales process seems like a conversation you have with a friend, it is easier, more fun, and the sale is on firmer ground.

Now we can move on to the practical application. How do we Clarify the Prospect's stated objection?

**Questions** drive the Clarification process, so let's begin with a basic introduction to questions. Questions are a recurring theme in this program, and when you use my subsequent books, you will have a master class on this subject. For now, at its most fundamental level, questions can be divided into two types: open and closed.

**Open questions** start a conversation because they require an explanation to answer them, while **closed questions** shut the conversation down, as they can only be answered with a "yes" or a "no." As a general rule, you should eliminate closed questions from your repertoire because they negatively impact the sales process.

For example, the Prospect might object to granting you an appointment by saying, "I'm already under contract with someone else for that." How might you respond if you were limited to only asking closed questions?

**Salesman**- "So you don't even want to hear what I have to offer?"

**Salesman**- "So you can't work with me even if you wanted to?"

**Salesman**- "Can we meet anyway so you have an option when the time comes for renewal?"

These responses range from horrible to cringeworthy.

When you use closed questions like these, you open yourself up to the risk of receiving a "No," and in this case, a "No" is the same thing as getting kicked out for life. Why take the chance when you don't have to?

On the other hand, open questions are highly encouraged, especially when it comes to Clarifying the Prospect's objection. Typically, they are identified as questions beginning with who, what, where, when, why, and how. Although these questions can potentially be answered with a single word, "No" is not one of them, and that's the one word we don't want to come out of the Prospect's mouth.

Let's revisit our appointment objection and see the difference open questions can make.

**Prospect**- "I'm already under contract with someone else for that."

**Salesman**- "Understood. Who are you working with?"

**Salesman**- "Great. What program did you go with?"

**Salesman**- "Glad to hear you have that covered. When does the contract come up for renewal?"

**Salesman**- "Fair enough. Where is their support team located these days?"

**Salesman**- "OK, if you don't mind me asking, how has the response been with them so far?"

How does this set of questions make the Prospect feel as compared to the previous set?

The reaction is going to be 180 degrees different. Instead of being despondent, we are inquisitive. Instead of being angry, we are supportive. And instead of getting banned for life, we have a high probability of establishing a relationship.

In each example, the Salesman throws out a quick word or phrase to indicate he has heard the objection and is abandoning his pursuit of the appointment, then he asks a benign probing question. Depending upon the Prospect's mood, he may ask a question about his decision which helps us build credibility, we may find a chink in the armor we can exploit, or the door may open for a future appointment.

Of all the open question types, there is one that is almost too powerful to use and that is the *Why* question. Why? Well, usually it signals the beginning of an argument. It sounds accusatory. You are asking the Prospect to defend his position. He doesn't owe you an explanation. You invaded his space and took up his time. If you failed to make your case, that's not his problem.

Besides open questions, there a couple question types that are useful in the Clarification process. The first one is the **Echo Technique**. The Echo Technique? Yes, the Echo Technique is when someone issues you an objection and you repeat it back to them in the form of a question.

In the form of a question? Yes, when they hear their own objection asked back to them, it lets them know you don't understand it as stated, so they are compelled to reissue it with more details. As their True Objection is already top of mind, they usually begin divulging specifics relating to it, which firms up the cloud and gives us something to work with.

The beauty of this technique is that if it's employed with a smile, it is very disarming and feels natural, not like a sales technique. For example:

**Prospect**- "It costs too much."

**Salesperson**- "It costs too much?"

**Prospect**- "Well, yeah, your competition prints 30,000 for the same price you guys want for 10,000."

**Prospect**- "It costs too much."

**Salesperson**- "It costs too much?"

**Prospect**- "Yeah, I have money in the budget, but not enough for this."

**Prospect**- "It costs too much."

**Salesperson**- "It costs too much?"

**Prospect**- "Seems like it. At that rate, I'm not too sure I can recoup my investment. Is there a way to try it out for less money?"

In each example, we came away with a specific, True objection.

My go-to clarification question is, "What do you mean by that?"

Without any context, the above question can sound a bit threatening, but if I told you it was said with a big smile and engaging body language, how would it come off? Friendly, inquisitive, and considerate.

**Salesperson-** "What do you mean by that?"

This is an excellent Clarification question for almost any stated objection, and I use it all the time, but I did have to practice it a bit before it became comfortable because I was concerned it would be too strong a reply. It has never failed me and to date has not produced a negative reaction, so hopefully, you can add this to your toolbox as well.

## ACKNOWLEDGE

Acknowledging is the step where you validate the Prospect's concern, and it is the most frequently skipped step in the communication process.

For example, let's say you've Clarified "We tried it once and it didn't work" down to:

**Prospect**- "It was another company we tried last year. We worked with them for a few months, but our revenue didn't go up. I cancelled the contract, saved the monthly fee, and our sales are still the same. It may work for other companies, but it doesn't work for us."

**Salesperson**- "I understand. What they proposed to you made sense, but when it came down to it, they couldn't deliver more sales. Very disappointing."

**Prospect**- "Well, that's kind of where I'm at."

That's it. You tell them you understand and prove it to them by reiterating their point.

This is you taking the thorn out of the tiger's paw. The Prospect wants to vent, so let him, because the more crap he gives you that he knows you don't deserve, the more willing he will be to let you answer the objection.

Because Prospects are concerned that sharing their True objection with you will hurt your feelings, they will be expecting a negative response from you. Acknowledging the objection absolves them of those fears and allows the conversation to move forward.

Zig Ziglar famously said, "All people want two things: to be heard and to be right."

When a Salesperson fires off a rebuttal the moment he hears an objection, the Prospect feels frustrated, as if his words had no value, or worse, were not even heard. To maintain rapport and keep the tone conversational, you must give the same weight of respect that you desire to wield. Just like you do not want to be rejected out of pocket, you must resist the temptation to do the same to the Prospect.

**Salesperson**- "I see. So from your perspective, my competition is offering you three times the value."

**Prospect**- "Exactly."

**Salesperson**- "I completely understand. If our media was the same as my competition and they offered three times the value, I'd be working for them. No question."

Can you feel the relief on the part of the Prospect when you read the Salesperson's words? This is Acknowledging. The Prospect is thinking, "Ah, he understands. He's not crazy. He's not trying to mislead me. He's letting me off the hook."

When you acknowledge someone's concern, you are in effect telling them:

**Salesperson**- "I am not mad, disappointed, or frustrated, and you shouldn't be either."

**Salesperson**- "You're not misguided. Your point of view has merit."

**Salesperson**- "I am listening and your message is understood. I do not put myself above you in this relationship."

**Salesperson**- "I have the ability to empathize with you. I am not pushing my thought process onto you."

Acknowledging is very gratifying to the Prospect; it's something they do not often receive from friends, family, coworkers, or even from the barista who screwed up his order this morning. It is a warm, fuzzy feeling and everyone wants more of it. It also earns you the right to speak next and motivates the Prospect to listen to you without having his guard up.

When you skip this step, you are committing to an adversarial relationship like playing tennis with words: both of you are running down what the other guy shot at you, both of you are slamming your message back over the net, and both of you are trying to score at the other's expense. It is a fast exchange that hurts rapport and is a departure from the Communication Model.

It would be better to treat the conversation like a game of catch in the backyard which is a good analogy for the Communication Model.

## COMMUNICATION MODEL

In the **Communication Model**, two people alternate being the Sender and the Receiver of messages just like when you play catch.

Before you throw the ball, make sure the other guy is ready to receive it; otherwise, you might make him drop his beer in surprise. It's the same in NNP and by extension CALM, where you prepare and wait for your partner to be motivated to listen to you.

Once he's ready, state your message. It is the receiver's responsibility to Acknowledge the message was received which could be in the form of body language, an affirmation, or an iteration like we are teaching here. An outward response is necessary to affirm what's happening in the mind of the Receiver. In the backyard, the Acknowledgement is more obvious because we can both see and hear the ball being caught.

Now roles reverse, and the Receiver becomes the Sender and vice versa. When you're playing catch, you have a clear picture of which role you are currently playing because there is only one ball. Whoever has the ball is now the Sender, the exchanges go back and forth in a uniform way, and we all get along.

Most conversations are in a social environment. When your partner is your friend, you have a very good frame of reference to work with, so misunderstandings are minimized.

You can skip the Clarifying and Acknowledging steps and still be simpatico. In business, especially when dealing with an objection, you need to cover your bases and work the fundamentals; otherwise, you run the risk of metaphorically spilling the Prospect's beer with your poor communication skills.

We Clarify to demonstrate we are listening, and we Acknowledge to ask permission to switch roles. If we Acknowledge properly, the Prospect understands he no longer needs to explain himself, and will be ready to play the role of Receiver.

# LEAD

So far, we have Clarified the objection down to specifics and Acknowledged its validity which earns us the right to answer it. When you boil it down, objections are nothing more than requests for more information.

Leading is both the answering of this request and the tone you employ while sharing new information. You should proceed with compassion and strength, the same as you would when teaching your teenager how to drive. You are not patronizing them, but you are also firm in your attachment to the truth.

Below are some techniques you can use to set up your response. Some of these may already be familiar to you, but they are usually presented as being the answers themselves and not a part of the communication process which is, in fact, what they really are.

## FEEL-FELT-FOUND

Let's begin with **Feel-Felt-Found** because we've already begun this process. Feel-Felt-Found, or FFF for short, is a three-step process where you agree with the Prospect, validate his concern, and share your personal story of how you transitioned from holding the same opinion the Prospect just expressed to the new one you have now.

**Salesperson**- "I know how you feel. I felt the same way until I found (insert game-changing fact here)."

**Salesperson**- "I know how you feel. I felt the same way for a long time until I found a service that delivers the exact same results for less money."

I ran a sales training class one time when one of the corporate VPs came in and asked to lead the module on FFF. He got up there and started talking about FFF. Every hand in the room immediately shot up. One lady couldn't wait to be called on and she spouted off,

**Negative Nancy**- "This doesn't work. That trick is like 10 years old. Everybody knows it. If you try something like that in my territory, they will kick you out and you'll never be welcome back again."

Without hesitation, my buddy says,

**Eddie Spaghetti**- "Look, I understand. I get it. We used to teach this way back in the 80s when I was a trainer for Dale

Carnegie. Even then, we all thought it was too canned of a response to actually work in the field, so what we did, instead of trashing this technique entirely, was train the students to put it in their own words. It worked because the psychological principles of empathizing, agreeing, and answering that underpin this technique still work. People are hard-wired to accept it positively."

Everyone was nodding in bovine agreement as they waited for him to give them an example. Meanwhile, I was standing in the back of the room cracking up. The students started turning around to look at me, and they were wondering what I found so funny about that exchange. Some of you may already have picked up on this as you're reading, but none of them did, until I pointed out my friend had just pulled FFF on all of them. They were telling him it wouldn't work, he threw it back in their faces, it worked, and they didn't even realize that he used it. Classic.

As we have already Acknowledged the Prospect's concern, we have basically told him, "I know how you feel." The remainder of this technique flows naturally.

To my friend's point, you should match all techniques to your personal style, and this means talking the way you normally do.

Instead of saying "I know how you feel," you might try:

**Salesperson**- "I understand."

**Salesperson**- "I get it."

**Salesperson**- "That makes complete sense."

Instead of saying "I felt the same way," you could say:

**Salesperson**- "That was my belief too for a long time."

**Salesperson**- "Everybody thought the same way."

**Salesperson**- "That was a problem for me too."

For the transition, instead of "until I found," you might opt for:

**Salesperson**- "until I learned"

**Salesperson**- "until my friend told me"

**Salesperson**- "then I looked into it and saw"

**Salesperson**- "because of that, the company changed to"

## REVERSAL

The next technique is the **Reversal**. We use this technique when the Prospect just flat mistakes a positive for a negative. This is when you essentially hold the mirror up to his face and reverse the objection.

**Salesperson**- "That's exactly why you SHOULD do business with me."

**Salesperson**- "If price is your concern, our program should be the most attractive to you."

Be careful not to spike the ball when using this technique. If your response sounds celebratory or frustrated, the Prospect will be emotionally tied to stand firm in his position. If you conduct yourself in a matter-of-fact way, the pill is much easier to swallow.

**Salesperson**- "So you like my competitor because their machine comes with a good warranty?"

**Prospect**- "Yes, I need to be able to budget my expenses, so I can't have breakdowns costing me unforeseen repairs."

**Salesperson**- "I completely understand, and this is actually one of our selling features. By leasing the machine through us, you are not responsible for any repairs. We take care of that, plus, you don't have to buy the machine up front. You just pay the monthly fee, which is better for your accounting."

## IF I COULD,..WOULD YOU,..

The third technique is the **If I Could Would You**, or IICWY. You may be using this in your prospecting already. Think of this proposal like a scale where you offer a lot of value (or weight) on one side in exchange for a relatively lighter expense of time on the other.

**Salesperson-** "If I could show you how to cut your expenses by $200 a week, would that be worth 20 minutes of your time to learn how?"

If used as a transition into Leading, this can motivate your Prospect to listen, because you are offering them something you know they want.

**Salesperson-** "If I can prove to you that I can bring you one more sale a week, would you be interested?"

## PRUDENT BUSINESS OWNER

The fourth commonly used technique is the **Prudent Business Owner**, when you dangle a compliment in exchange for time.

**Salesperson-** "As a prudent business owner, I'm sure you want to know all your options before you make a choice, right?"

If they say "yes," well then, they are prudent business owners, and if they say "no," they are not. The carrot and the stick.

**Salesperson**- "I work with some of the best companies in the region, and I have for a long time because I consistently make them money. If you are serious about growing your business, and I gather you are, would it make sense to see what we have to offer?"

## JUST ASK

The fifth technique isn't a technique at all. This is what I promised you at the beginning of this program. All four of the previous techniques were crutches to make it easier for you to ask permission to take on the role of Sender, so why not just do that?

**Salesperson-** "I understand your concern. I have an answer for that. Would it be ok if I shared that with you?"

**Salesperson-** "Yes, all of my clients have the same concern. The difference is they decided to work with me and continue to do so. Can I briefly tell you why?"

That's it. Nothing to memorize. Just be polite and ask for permission. They'll agree, and they always agree. Why?

Because courtesy begets courtesy. That's enough right there, but there is an added value because you are, in effect, lowering yourself in front of the Prospect by deliberately *requesting* the right to speak. You may have been having a conversation for the last 20 minutes for all I know, but when you ask for permission, you empower the Prospect. People love to feel powerful, so they agree.

Let's say the Prospect offers an objection based on some minutia you have never even heard of, and you don't know how to respond. Don't worry. It's ok. You don't have to have an answer for everything.

When I something is thrown at me from left field, I will put my hands up and say, "Good question. I don't know, but I will find out. If I get a good answer, I'll come back and let you know."

You need to protect your reputation at all costs, so resist the temptation to BS the Prospect. If you lie, you'll get caught, and it will follow you. If you don't know, be honest and have the courage to admit it.

> **LAW #7:**
> You don't have to be right about everything;
> just don't be wrong about anything.

# MOVE ON

We guided the Prospect from Negative to Neutral which was the hard part of the process. Inserting the Positive is very easy, because the Prospect is motivated to hear it.

Have you ever heard of the Four Levels of Learning? They are:

1. Unconscious Incompetence
2. Conscious Incompetence
3. Conscious Competence
4. Unconscious Competence

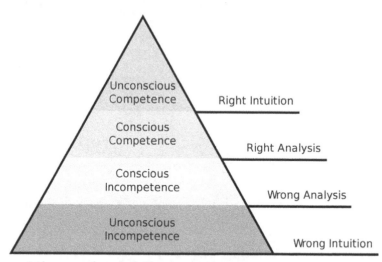

## Hierarchy of Competence

*Competence Hierarchy adapted from Noel Burch by Igor Kokcharov.jpg by Kokcharov*

When you were a toddler, your mother probably told you to tie your shoelaces several times, but the first time, your response was, "What are shoelaces?"

Prior to this question, you were unconsciously incompetent when it came to tying shoelaces, meaning you were not aware (unconscious) that you couldn't do something (incompetent). You didn't even know what shoelaces were much less how to tie them. When your mom pointed to your shoes and said, "Those are shoelaces," you became aware (conscious) that you didn't know something (incompetent).

This is a very motivating state of mind to be in, so you quickly learned how to tie your shoelaces. In the beginning, you needed to concentrate (conscious) on the mechanics of tying the shoelaces in order to get them tied correctly (competent). In a couple weeks, you were able to do it without thinking. This is when you reached the fourth level. You didn't have to think about it (unconscious) to do it correctly (competent).

When you bring someone from Negative to Neutral, they have moved from Unconscious Incompetence (they didn't know they were wrong) to the state of Conscious Incompetence (they are aware they were wrong but don't yet know what is right). As a result, they are very motivated to build an informed opinion on the subject quickly.

They are all ears. They abdicate the role of Speaker and assume the mantle of Listener. All our training so far culminates to this inflexion point, so yes, the next step is easy.

You give them one Positive about your product, and they will be at Positive.

I want to punctuate something here. Traditional sales theory instructs us to *begin* our objection handling process with the insertion of positives, also known as Features and Benefits. Knowing what you know now, how successful do you think you'd be if you skipped these first three steps?

Not very. Seems amateur at this point, doesn't it?

Moving On takes us from Neutral to Positive, and it also refers to progressing the sale. This is where I tell you to expect to win and to trust the process. See, there is a rhythm you set and a momentum you build throughout your sales track, and it was interrupted with the objection you just handled. You need to continue down your sales path as if nothing happened, because if you hesitate, it will expose your lack of confidence in your response. If the Prospect even suspects you think your answer was weak, how can he have faith in it?

All your work and rapport will be flushed down the toilet in the blink of an eye.

When you get right back to your story, it implies this is business as usual, and this has an extreme psychological impact. Your Prospect will conclude that you have encountered this many times; it's no big deal, and all the previous scenarios ended up the same way, with a sale. This is called **Implied Peer Pressure** and it is very powerful.

If the Prospect resists at this point, in his mind, he is not just opposing you, he is opposing everyone who has ever addressed this concern. If all of them agreed to buy, maybe he's wrong to remain apprehensive.

The opposite will actually occur. He will become *more* willing to buy, because making the same conclusion as countless others gives him peace of mind. He is making the right decision; this is a hidden benefit of NNP.

In other objection handling models, the Prospect is a bit damaged after he acquiesces, because the Salesman beat him in an argument or overloaded him and suffocated his objection. He's not happy.

With our system, the Prospect becomes excited because he learned something and has confidence. He knows he is doing something positive, so don't hesitate. Get right back on track.

## PARTING THOUGHT

You're walking through your home, you turn the corner into a hallway, and you see a chair right there in the middle of the hall.

What is your first reaction? How does that make you feel?

Most of us are going to be mad.

This chair is blocking the hallway!

What is that chair doing there?

Who left it there?

Why didn't they put that back where it belongs?

Am I the only one who cares about how this house looks?

Now step back and consider this.

Maybe you get tired and that chair is there to give you a rest.

Maybe you need it to stand on to change the lightbulb.

Maybe you thought you lost it, and now it's found.

Maybe who cares? You could walk to the right of it, to the left of it, go under it, or jump over it.

NNP should teach you that nothing is negative or positive in itself. It is all in how you choose to perceive it, and how you choose to utilize it, so the next time you react to something negatively, step back and ask yourself, "What can I use this for? What can I learn from this?"

*I __Thank You__ for buying my book,
and wish you the best!*

For public speaking bookings, private consultations, or just to keep in touch, please visit us online at JiuJitsuSelling.com or on our Facebook page. If you liked this book, please give us a positive review and go buy my next book.

CPSIA information can be obtained
at www.ICGtesting.com
Printed in the USA
LVHW012040010820
662079LV00018B/399

9 781735 377100